Israel

JOY GREGORY

MEDIA ENHANCED BOOKS

AV2
BY WEIGL

ADDED VALUE • AUDIO VISUAL

www.av2books.com

AV² provides enriched content that supplements and complements this book. Weigl's AV² books strive to create inspired learning and engage young minds in a total learning experience.

Your AV² Media Enhanced books come alive with...

Audio
Listen to sections of the book read aloud.

Key Words
Study vocabulary, and complete a matching word activity.

Video
Watch informative video clips.

Quizzes
Test your knowledge.

Go to **www.av2books.com**, and enter this book's unique code.

BOOK CODE

M729194

Embedded Weblinks
Gain additional information for research.

Slide Show
View images and captions, and prepare a presentation.

AV² by Weigl brings you media enhanced books that support active learning.

Try This!
Complete activities and hands-on experiments.

... and much, much more!

Published by AV² by Weigl
350 5th Avenue, 59th Floor
New York, NY 10118
Websites: www.av2books.com   www.weigl.com

Library of Congress Cataloging-in-Publication Data

Gregory, Joy.
  Israel / Joy Gregory. — (Exploring countries)
    pages cm. — (Exploring countries)
  Includes index.
  ISBN 978-1-4896-1014-0 (hardcover : alk. paper) — ISBN 978-1-4896-1015-7 (softcover : alk. paper) —
ISBN 978-1-4896-1016-4 (single user ebk.) — ISBN 978-1-4896-1017-1 (multi user ebk.)
  1. Israel—Juvenile literature. I. Title.
  DS126.5.G676 2014
  956.94—dc23
                  2014005942

Printed in the United States of America in North Mankato, Minnesota
1 2 3 4 5 6 7 8 9 0 18 17 16 15 14

042014
WEP150314

Project Coordinator Heather Kissock
Art Director Terry Paulhus

Photo Credits
Every reasonable effort has been made to trace ownership and to obtain permission to reprint copyright material. The publishers would be pleased to have any errors or omissions brought to their attention so that they may be corrected in subsequent printings.

Weigl acknowledges Getty Images as its primary image supplier for this title.

Contents

Israel Overview

Israel is a **democratic** country located in the Middle East, a region of western Asia and North Africa. Established by the **United Nations** in 1948, Israel is the only Jewish nation in the world. Although Israel is a young country, its land has a long history, going back thousands of years. The creation of Israel on land with historic ties to both Jews and Arabs has led to armed conflict between Israel and its Arab neighbors. Israel and some of its neighbors continue to disagree over Israel's borders.

Markets in Tel Aviv-Yafo and other cities are popular places to shop for fresh fruits and vegetables.

The Tel Aviv Museum of Art has one of Israel's largest collections of paintings and other artworks.

Israel has the world's largest diamond cutting and polishing industry.

Ostriches are bred at the Hai-Bar Nature Reserve, one of many areas set aside to protect plant and animal life.

Soccer, better known as football in Israel, is the country's most popular sport.

Israel 5

Exploring
Israel

Israel is a narrow country with a western border that stretches 115 miles (185 kilometers) along the eastern coast of the Mediterranean Sea. The country is only 85 miles (135 km) wide at its widest point. Israel borders Lebanon to the north and Syria to the northeast. The country shares its eastern border with Jordan and the area known as the West Bank. On the southwest, Israel borders Egypt and the area called Gaza. The southern tip of Israel touches the Gulf of Aqaba, which is at the northern end of the Red Sea. Slightly smaller than the U.S. state of New Jersey, Israel covers a total area of 8,019 square miles (20,770 square kilometers).

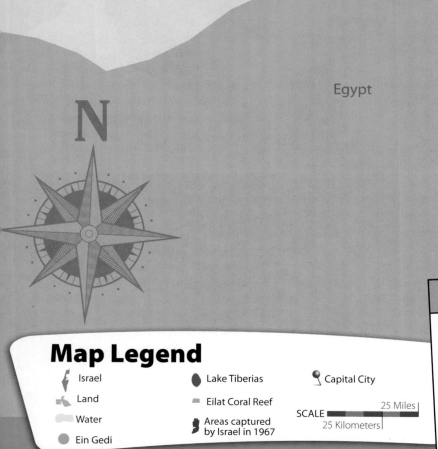

Egypt

Eilat Coral Reef

Map Legend

Israel	Lake Tiberias	Capital City
Land	Eilat Coral Reef	
Water	Areas captured by Israel in 1967	
Ein Gedi		

SCALE

25 Miles

25 Kilometers

Eilat Coral Reef

A coral reef that is about 4,000 feet (1,200 meters) long lies near the shore of the Gulf of Aqaba, close to the resort city of Eilat. Now a nature reserve, the reef provides a home for more than 270 coral **species** and thousands of other types of sea life. The area is popular with divers and other tourists.

Lebanon

Syria

Golan Heights

Lake Tiberias

Mediterranean Sea

West Bank

Jerusalem

Jerusalem

Dead Sea

Jordan

Gaza

I S R A E L

Egypt

Ein Gedi

Saudi Arabia

Lake Tiberias

Lake Tiberias is Israel's largest lake containing freshwater. Most of its water comes from the Jordan River. The lake is also known as the Sea of Galilee.

Ein Gedi

Ein Gedi is an **oasis** in southeastern Israel. Much of the land around the oasis is now a nature reserve. Hundreds of species of plants, birds, and other animals live in the reserve.

Jerusalem

Jerusalem is the capital of Israel. The city is about 5,000 years old. It includes a number of sites that are considered sacred by Jews, Christians, and Muslims, or people who follow Islam.

LAND AND CLIMATE

The Negev Desert receives only 2 to 4 inches (5 to 10 centimeters) of rain each year.

Although Israel is a small country, it has four geographic regions. Along the Mediterranean Sea, the western side of Israel is a coastal plain with fertile soil that is good for growing crops. To the east of this plain are the central highlands. Small fertile valleys and barren hills can be found there. Located east of the highlands is the Jordan Rift Valley. It includes the area around the Jordan River, the Dead Sea, and Lake Tiberias. The fourth region is the Negev Desert. This triangular-shaped region is about 4,700 square miles (12,000 sq. km) in size and covers most of southern Israel.

The Dead Sea is a saltwater lake on the border of Israel and Jordan. It is about 50 miles (80 km) long and up to 11 miles (18 km) wide. The lake is 1,300 feet (400 m) below sea level, making it the lowest spot on the surface of Earth.

Israel has two distinct seasons. The cool, rainy winter lasts from November to May. The hot, dry summer occurs between June and October.

Temperatures in Israel vary according to the region. Along the Mediterranean Sea, daytime temperatures range from 84° Fahrenheit (29° Celsius) in August to about 61°F (16°C) in January. In the southern city of Eilat, high temperatures range from 103°F (39°C) in August to 70°F (21°C) in January. Jerusalem, located in the highlands, is cooler. Temperatures range from about 75°F (24°C) in August to about 50°F (10°C) in January, and there may be snow during the winter.

Many types of wildflowers grow in nature reserves near Lake Tiberias.

12 Ounces per Quart
Concentration of salt in the Dead Sea. (340 grams per liter)

129°F Highest temperature ever recorded in Israel, at Tirat Zvi on June 21, 1942. (54°C)

3,963 Feet
Height of Mount Meron, the highest peak in Israel. (1,208 m)

PLANTS AND ANIMALS

Israel has more than 100 kinds of land mammals, including gazelles, wild boars, and Nubian ibex. Wooded areas are home to foxes and wolves. Leopards are sometimes seen. Reptile species found in Israel include geckos, lizards, and vipers.

Many types of birds have been identified in Israel. Pelicans, honey buzzards, coots, and starlings spend the winter months there. Sylvia warblers and goldcrests live in Israel throughout the year.

The coastal waters of the Gulf of Aqaba contain many species of fish and shellfish. Whale sharks and dolphins are common in the area. Hawksbill sea turtles nest on Eilat's beaches.

More than 2,800 kinds of plants are found in Israel. Hills in the coastal region are covered with **maquis**. Israel is the northernmost place where papyrus reeds grow. The ancient Egyptians used these reeds to make paper. Wild desert scrub, pistachios, and date palms grow in the Negev Desert.

Honeysuckle and large plane trees cover hilly areas near Lake Tiberias. Neot Kedumim is a nature reserve located between Tel Aviv-Yafo and Jerusalem. It collects and conserves plants mentioned in the Bible.

Plants and Animals BY THE NUMBERS

More Than 400
Number of bird species that live in Israel.

1956 Year that the Israeli government began to protect Eilat's coral reef.

135 Varieties of butterflies found in Israel.

Mountain gazelles can be found in the hilly areas of northern Israel. Excellent runners, they can reach speeds of 50 miles (80 km) per hour.

NATURAL RESOURCES

Compared to other countries in the Middle East, Israel is not rich in natural resources. However, it does produce some minerals and other resources that help its **economy**. The Dead Sea is a source of potash, which is used in fertilizer. Magnesium bromide, used in medications, also comes from the Dead Sea. Mud from the Dead Sea is used as a beauty product.

Minerals produced in Israel also include gypsum and marble. Copper ore is mined in southern Israel. Sand is used to make glass, cement, and other products.

Historically, Israel has used coal and oil to generate electricity. In recent years, however, the country has begun to rely more on natural gas as an energy source. In 2009, large natural gas deposits were discovered in the Mediterranean off the Israeli coast. Israel is developing this resource.

Water is a natural resource that is in short supply. The country gets freshwater from Lake Tiberias and from several **aquifers**. Israel also has developed other water sources. **Desalination** plants turn seawater into freshwater. Treatment plants are able to clean wastewater so that it can be used again.

Potash removed from Dead Sea water is sent to large storage facilities. Then, it is shipped worldwide.

TOURISM

People from around the world visit Israel. Many want to tour Israel's varied historical and religious sites. The country's warm climate attracts tourists to its beaches and to outdoor activities that include hiking, biking, and windsurfing.

Health tourism is a big business in Israel. Some health tourists spend time at **spas** that use mineral-rich mud from the Dead Sea. Visitors believe this mud can make the skin look younger and may have health benefits. Many tourists also like to experience floating in the Dead Sea, where the water's high salt content makes it very easy for a person to stay afloat.

Thousands of tourists from Europe and other areas enjoy Eilat's warm weather and opportunities for water sports each winter.

The Dead Sea area also features many historical sites. These include **archaeological** sites at Qumran. The Dead Sea scrolls, found at Qumran, contain the world's oldest Bible, and they help researchers understand early **Christianity**. Ancient monasteries built on cliff walls near the Dead Sea are also popular with tourists.

Masada is an ancient fortress. Jews rebelling against Roman rule made a last stand there, fighting a Roman army in 72–73 AD. In 2001, Masada was named a World Heritage Site by **UNESCO**.

Masada is located on a mountain that towers 1,424 feet (434 m) above the Dead Sea. It took almost 15,000 Roman soldiers nearly two years to defeat fewer than 1,000 Jewish defenders.

Jerusalem attracts millions of tourists every year. The oldest part of Jerusalem is called the Old City. Inside the Old City are many holy sites. These include the Western Wall, which is sacred to Jews. The Western Wall is all that remains of the Second Temple, a Jewish house of worship that was destroyed by Roman soldiers in 70 AD.

Christians believe the Church of the Holy Sepulchre in the Old City marks the place where Jesus Christ was crucified and buried. The Dome of the Rock is a holy site for Muslims. They believe it is where Muhammad, Islam's founder, rose into heaven.

Israel is also home to about 270 kibbutzim. A kibbutz is a community where people live and work together and all wealth is shared. Kibbutzim often welcome visitors to tour their operations. Some allow visitors to stay overnight or for longer periods.

More than 10 million people go to the Western Wall each year. They include Israelis and visitors from many other countries.

MORE THAN 3 MILLION

Number of tourists who visit Israel each year.

2,000 Years Old

Age of the Tomb of Absalom, a monument in an ancient cemetery on the Mount of Olives, near Jerusalem's Old City.

INDUSTRY

Manufacturing is important to Israel's economy. Many of the goods manufactured in Israel are high-technology items. These include electronics products, computer hardware, communications systems, and medical instruments.

The country's well-educated population has helped the growth of high-tech industries. As of 2011, 45 percent of Israelis had at least some college education, a higher portion than any other country in the world except Canada. Israel has benefited over the years from receiving many highly educated **immigrants** from areas such as Europe and the United States.

In addition to high-tech items, other products manufactured in Israel include building materials, chemicals, medications, food products, **textiles**, and clothing. Many of Israel's kibbutzim raise crops and make food products. However, some produce other goods, including machinery and items made from plastics or rubber.

A number of Israel's manufacturing industries are based in or near Haifa. This city on the Mediterranean coast has the country's largest seaport. A location near the seaport helps companies **export** some of what they produce.

Large printing machines that use the latest technology are manufactured in Israel.

GOODS AND SERVICES

More than 80 percent of workers in Israel are employed in service industries. These are industries in which workers provide a service to other people, rather than produce goods. Many service workers in Israel are employed in the banking industry. Others work for companies that provide services for tourists. Service workers also include doctors and nurses, teachers, and people who work in stores and restaurants.

Only about 2 percent of Israeli workers earn their living in agriculture. A great deal of the country is desert or **semi-arid**, and less that 15 percent of the land is suitable for farming. The country's main agricultural products include citrus fruits, vegetables, and cotton.

Although Israel exports some of the fruits and vegetables it grows, the country needs to **import** other types of food items. Israel also imports oil, used for fuel and to make chemicals. The countries a nation imports from and exports to are called its trading partners. Israel's largest trading partner is the United States, followed by China.

1985
Year the new shekel, the type of money now used in Israel, was introduced.

28%
Portion of Israeli exports sold to the United States.

3.6 Million
Number of workers in Israel.

Olives, fruits, and vegetables are some of the crops grown in the Jezreel Valley in northern Israel.

INDIGENOUS PEOPLES

Archaeologists have found evidence that **indigenous** peoples lived in the region that includes Israel as early as 10,000 years ago. Both Jews and Arabs claim the region as their native land. Jewish people trace their history in the area back to Abraham. He was the founder of Judaism, the Jewish faith, more than 3,000 years ago. At that time, Jewish people called the region Canaan. Jews believe Canaan was promised to them by God.

Arabs also trace their presence in the area back for thousands of years. Most Arabs adopted the Islamic faith following the founding of that religion in the 7th century AD. In addition, the Druze people have been living in the area for centuries. The Druze practice a religion that developed in the 11th century. The **nomadic** Bedouin people have also been in the region since ancient times.

Indigenous Peoples BY THE NUMBERS

175 Number of years Abraham is said to have lived, according to Jewish tradition.

ABOUT 125,000 Number of Druze people now living in Israel.

25% Portion of Israel's current population that is Arab.

Many Bedouins in Israel herd animals such as goats, sheep, and camels.

THE AGE OF EXPLORATION

The area that is now Israel has seen many conflicts over the centuries. Beginning about 2,600 years ago, the region was conquered by a series of foreign empires. Foreign rulers included the Babylonians, Persians, and Greeks. The Babylonians **deported** many Jews into slavery. This event is often considered the beginning of the Diaspora, the scattering of the Jewish people to many other areas of the world.

The Romans took control of what is now Israel in 63 BC. They crushed several revolts over the next few centuries. In 313 AD, the region became part of the Byzantine Empire, which ruled the area until the 700s, when Muslim Arabs took control.

The Ottoman Empire, based in Turkey, ruled the region from 1516 until 1918, when World War I ended. After the war, a new international organization called the League of Nations gave Great Britain temporary control of the region, which was then called Palestine. The League's intention was that Palestine would later become independent.

During a series of wars known as the Crusades, Christian soldiers from Europe captured Jerusalem for a time in the 11th century.

EARLY SETTLERS

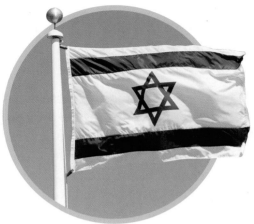

The flag of Israel was adopted in 1948. The Star of David on the flag is named for a Jewish king who lived around 1000 BC.

A small number of Jews remained in Palestine over the centuries. This number began to grow in the late 1800s and early 1900s. **Anti-Semitism** was increasing in Europe, where many Jews were living at the time. The Zionist movement was born in response. This was a movement to create a Jewish state in the land where Jewish people trace their beginnings. Many Arabs in Palestine opposed Jewish immigration, and Arab leaders persuaded the British to halt it. However, some Jewish people continued to slip into Palestine.

Persecution of European Jews increased after the Nazi government led by Adolf Hitler came to power in Germany in the 1930s. During World War II, millions of Jews in Europe were killed by the Nazis, an event that became known as the Holocaust. After the war, many European Jews who survived wished to move to Palestine. Support for creating a Jewish state there increased in many nations around the world.

Thousands of Jewish immigrants arrived in Israel from Europe by ship in the years after World War II.

The United Nations, which replaced the League of Nations, voted to divide Palestine into Jewish and Arab countries. Arabs in Palestine and neighboring nations opposed this action. When Israel became independent in 1948, Arab countries attacked it. Israel defeated the attackers.

Since 1948, Israel has fought wars with its neighbors in 1956, 1967, and 1973. In the 1967 war, Israel captured the West Bank from Jordan, Gaza from Egypt, and the region called the Golan Heights from Syria. Israel still controls the Golan Heights, and some Israeli Jews have moved into the area. In 2005, Israel removed all if its troops from Gaza, where there is now a Palestinian Arab government.

Jewish people from Israel have built many settlements in the West Bank. A large number of Arabs in the area are opposed to these settlements. In about half of the West Bank, Israel allows Palestinian Arabs to have autonomy, or local self-government.

The original country of Israel included only the western part of the city of Jerusalem. Israel captured East Jerusalem in the 1967 war. It still controls the entire city.

To prevent attacks on settlers, the Israeli government is building a fence in parts of the West Bank to separate Jewish settlements from Arab areas.

Early Settlers BY THE NUMBERS

6 Days
Length of the 1967 war between Israel and Arab countries, a conflict commonly known as the Six-Day War.

About 340,000
Number of Jewish settlers in the West Bank.

139 Square Miles
Area of Gaza, which has a population of 1.8 million Palestinian Arabs. (360 sq. km)

POPULATION

Israel has a population of 7.7 million people. Its population is notable for its diversity. Since 1948, 2.7 million Jews have moved to Israel from more than 100 countries.

In the 1990s, about 1 million people came to Israel from Russia. For almost 70 years, Russia had been part of the Union of Soviet Socialist Republics, or Soviet Union. Jews were victims of persecution in the Soviet Union. Some were allowed to go to Israel, but many were not permitted to leave the country. In 1991, when the Soviet Union broke up into Russia and several other countries, immigration became easier.

Thousands of Jews from the African country of Ethiopia became immigrants to Israel in the 1980s and 1990s. The Israeli government sent planes to countries bordering Ethiopia to pick up people fleeing persecution. As of 2012, about 5 percent of people living in Israel were born in Africa.

More than nine out of ten Israelis live in **urban** areas. The country's largest city is Tel Aviv-Yafo. Located on the Mediterranean coast, the city is home to about 3.3 million people. More than 1 million people live in Haifa, Israel's second-largest city.

Between 1989 and 1992, Israel's population grew by nearly 10 percent, due to Russian and Ethiopian immigration.

Population BY THE NUMBERS

790,000
Population of Jerusalem, Israel's third-largest city.

27%
Portion of the Israeli population that is under 15 years old.

1.5%
Rate at which Israel's population is increasing each year.

POLITICS AND GOVERNMENT

I srael's form of government is called a parliamentary democracy. Israeli citizens elect the members of the Knesset, the country's legislature. The Knesset, which has 120 members, makes Israel's laws.

The government is led by a prime minister, who is usually the leader of the political party that has the most seats, or members, in the Knesset. There are many political parties in Israel. As a result, it is difficult for one party to win a majority of Knesset seats and be able to pass laws on its own. Therefore, the prime minister needs to form a coalition government. In a coalition, two or more political parties agree to work together to pass laws.

The Knesset also elects Israel's president. The president appoints certain officials, including the justices of the country's Supreme Court. However, the prime minister has more power than the president to make government policies.

18 Years Age at which Israeli citizens can vote in elections.

1969–1974 Years that Golda Meir served as Israel's first female prime minister.

15 Number of judges on Israel's Supreme Court.

Members of the Knesset are elected for a term of up to four years. However, a new election may occur earlier if the prime minister loses an important vote in the legislature.

CULTURAL GROUPS

Israeli law allows people in the country to practice any religion they choose. Three-fourths of Israelis are Jewish. About 17 percent of the population is Muslim, and 2 percent of Israelis are Christian.

Religious practice varies among different groups of Jews in Israel. Ultra-Orthodox Jews believe that the religion's ancient sacred texts should be followed very closely. Orthodox rules regarding such things as religious services, clothing, diet, and the roles of men and women differ from the practices of other Jews.

The majority of Jewish Israelis believe that religious customs should be adapted to modern times. Some Jews in Israel do not practice their religion. They are known as secular Jews.

Signs in Israel are often written in three languages. They are Hebrew, Arabic, and English.

Many ultra-Orthodox Jewish men wear dark suits and top hats. They do not cut their beards or their side locks of hair.

Jews in Israel also have different cultural traditions depending on where they or their **ancestors** are from. People of European descent are called Ashkenazi Jews. Jews from Africa, the Middle East, and other parts of Asia are called Sephardic Jews.

Foods such as hummus, falafel, and couscous are enjoyed in many Mediterranean and Middle Eastern countries, and these foods are common in Israel. However, Ashkenazi Jewish immigrants have also brought to Israel traditional foods, music, and dance from countries such as Russia, Romania, Poland, and Hungary. Sephardic groups from Iraq, Iran, Yemen, and other countries have added their own traditional foods and customs to Israeli culture.

A modern form of Hebrew, the ancient language of the Jewish people, is the most common language spoken in Israel. Most Israeli Arabs speak Arabic. English is the most widely spoken foreign language, followed by Russian. Many Israelis speak Yiddish. This is a Germanic language used by Jewish people from Eastern and Central Europe.

Cultural Groups BY THE NUMBERS

1953 Year the government set up the Academy of the Hebrew Language, to approve new words and other changes in the language over time.

74% Portion of the Jewish population who are *sabras*, which means they were born in Israel.

200,000 Number of Israelis who speak Yiddish.

Chickpeas are used to make hummus, a pureed spread. Falafel is made using ground-up chickpeas and spices. The mixture is shaped into balls and fried.

ARTS AND ENTERTAINMENT

Israel has more than 230 museums. Some, such as the Israel Museum in Jerusalem, focus their collections on works of art and objects found by archaeologists. The Dead Sea Scrolls are in the Israel Museum. The Tel Aviv Museum of Art has a large collection of Israeli art, as well as works by European painters.

The MadaTech, Israel's National Museum of Science, Technology, and Space, is located in Haifa. It specializes in science-themed exhibits and 3D movies. The Museum for Islamic Art in Jerusalem displays one of the world's most important collections of Islamic art. The museum also has a collection of more than 180 antique watches. Exhibits at the Yad Vashem Holocaust History Museum in Jerusalem honor the memories of the 6 million people who died in the Holocaust.

A four-year project to enlarge and modernize the Habima Theater Building in Tel Aviv-Yafo was completed in 2012.

One part of Yad Vashem is the Hall of Names, where personal details about millions of Holocaust victims are recorded. The words *yad vashem* mean "as a place to memorialize."

Several of Israel's performing arts groups were established before the nation was formed. Israel's national theater, Habima, began in Moscow, Russia, in 1917. From the beginning, actors performed plays in Hebrew. In 1931, Habima was relocated to Tel Aviv-Yafo. The Israel Philharmonic Orchestra, which was first called the Palestine Orchestra, began performing in 1936.

Popular music in Israel is influenced by global trends. Israeli pop singers often perform in Hebrew, and the country's music scene includes festivals devoted to jazz, rock, and rap. It also includes klezmer concerts. Klezmer is a type of music associated with Jewish communities in Eastern Europe. The Safed Klezmer Festival features more than 100 performances. Klezmer is also part of the Desert Sounds Festival, held in the Negev Desert. That outdoor festival includes performances of many styles of music, including Israeli rock, traditional Arabic, and classical.

The Israel Philharmonic Orchestra performs both in Israel and around the world. Guest artists, such as Nitzan Bartana and Pinchas Zukerman, often accompany the orchestra.

SPORTS

There are hundreds of local soccer clubs in Israel, and many people enjoy both playing and watching the sport. Men's professional teams compete in the Israeli Premier League, and women's teams play in the Israeli Women's Premier League. Israel is a member of the Union of European Football Associations (UEFA), and its teams compete in UEFA international tournaments.

Shahar Peer of Israel had won nine Women's Tennis Association international tournaments by the end of 2013.

Basketball is also popular. The top 12 men's professional teams play in Ligat HaAl. The name means "super league." Nine professional women's teams compete in the D1 League, and there are other men's leagues. Israel's largest basketball stadium is located in Tel Aviv-Yafo. It is the home arena for Maccabi Electra Tel Aviv, the country's most successful basketball team. Maccabi Electra Tel Aviv plays in Ligat HaAl. Between 1954, when the league was started, and 2013, the team won the league championship 50 times.

Maccabi Electra Tel Aviv competes in European championships. Some of its players are from the United States.

In 1932, the first Maccabiah Games were held in the region, which was then under British control. The Maccabiah Games bring together Jewish athletes from all over the world. Athletes compete in more than two dozen sports, including track and field, swimming, basketball, and table tennis. Since 1953, the games have been held every four years. In recent years, the games have attracted thousands of athletes from more than 50 countries.

Israel sent its first Olympic team to the 1952 Olympics in Helsinki, Finland. Since then, seven Israeli athletes have won medals at the Olympic Games, in sailing, judo, and canoe sprint. Israeli athletes were the target of a terrorist attack at the 1972 Games in Munich, West Germany. Members of a Palestinian group called Black September kidnapped and killed 11 members of the Israeli team.

Mountain biking, scuba diving, tennis, and windsurfing are also popular in Israel. Eilat is a favorite destination for people who enjoy water sports. Mountain bikers can find trails in many parts of the country.

The Negev Desert is a popular destination for mountain bikers. Trails allow bikers to enjoy both their sport and the rugged beauty of the landscape.

Sports BY THE NUMBERS

14 Number of soccer teams that play in the Israeli Premier League.

2004 Year that Gal Fridman won Israel's only Olympic gold medal, in sailing.

23 Number of years in a row that Maccabi Electra Tel Aviv won the Ligat HaAl championship, from 1970 to 1992.

Mapping Israel

We use many tools to interpret maps and to understand the locations of features such as cities, states, lakes, and rivers. The map below has many tools to help interpret information on the map of Israel.

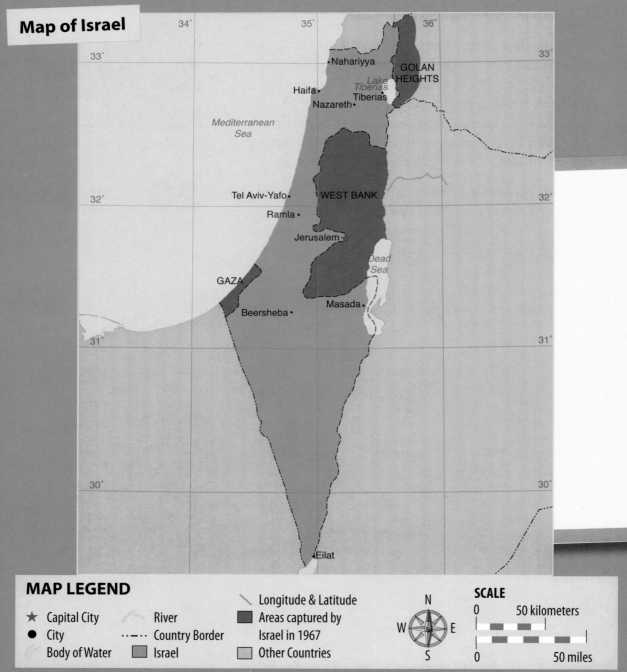

Map of Israel

MAP LEGEND

★ Capital City
● City
  Body of Water
  River
- · - · Country Border
  Israel

  Longitude & Latitude
  Areas captured by Israel in 1967
  Other Countries

SCALE
0   50 kilometers
0   50 miles

Mapping Tools

- The compass rose shows north, south, east, and west. The points in between represent northeast, northwest, southeast, and southwest.
- The map scale shows that the distances on a map represent much longer distances in real life. If you measure the distance between objects on a map, you can use the map scale to calculate the actual distance in miles or kilometers between those two points.

- The lines of latitude and longitude are long lines that appear on maps. The lines of latitude run east to west and measure how far north or south of the equator a place is located. The lines of longitude run north to south and measure how far east or west of the Prime Meridian a place is located. A location on a map can be found by using the two numbers where latitude and longitude meet. This number is called a coordinate and is written using degrees and direction. For example, the city of Eilat would be found at 29°N and 35°E on a map.

Map It!

Using the map and the appropriate tools, complete the activities below.

Locating with latitude and longitude
1. Which city is found at 32.8°N and 35°E?
2. Which lake is located at 32.8°N and 35.6°E?
3. Which ancient fortress is located at 31.3°N and 35.4°E?

Distances between points
4. Using the map scale and a ruler, calculate the approximate distance between the cities of Tel Aviv-Yafo and Beersheba.
5. What is the approximate width of Israel at the 31°N latitude?
6. Using the map scale and a ruler, find the approximate length of Israel from its northern tip on the Mediterranean Sea to Eilat in the south.

ANSWERS 1. Haifa 2. Lake Tiberias 3. Masada 4. about 65 miles (105 km) 5. 75 miles (120 km) 6. about 300 miles (485 km)

Quiz Time

Test your knowledge of Israel by answering these questions.

1 Which sea borders Israel's western edge?

2 In what year did Israel become an independent country?

3 What is the largest desert in Israel?

4 Which city has Israel's largest seaport?

5 What is the name of the movement that promoted the formation of a Jewish state?

6 What competition brings Jewish athletes from around the world to Israel every four years?

7 What is the most popular sport in Israel?

8 In what region is Israel located?

9 What is the population of Israel?

10 What is the highest temperature ever recorded in Israel?

ANSWERS

1. Mediterranean Sea
2. 1948
3. Negev Desert
4. Haifa
5. Zionism
6. Maccabiah Games
7. Soccer
8. Middle East
9. 7.7 million
10. 129°F (54°C)

Key Words

ancestors: members of a family who lived long ago

anti-Semitism: hatred of Jewish people as a group

aquifers: layers of rock and sand below the ground that can absorb and hold water

archaeological: related to the study of past human life using remains such as bones, tools, or writing left by ancient peoples

Christianity: a religion based on the teachings of Jesus Christ

democratic: a form of government in which people choose leaders by voting

deported: forced to leave a country or area

desalination: the process of removing salt from water

economy: the wealth and resources of a country or area

export: to send goods to another country for sale

immigrants: people who move to a new country or area to live and work

import: to bring in goods from another country

indigenous: native to a particular area

maquis: a short evergreen plant common along the shores of the Mediterranean Sea

nomadic: moving from place to place as a way of life

oasis: an area in a desert region that has a supply of water and where plants can grow well

persecution: treating a person or group of people harshly and unfairly on the basis of race, religion, or some other factor

semi-arid: having from 10 to 20 inches (25 to 50 cm) of rainfall a year

spas: resorts that people visit to improve their health and appearance

species: groups of living things with common characteristics

textiles: woven or knit cloth

UNESCO: the United Nations Educational, Scientific, and Cultural Organization, whose main goals are to promote world peace and eliminate poverty through education, science, and culture

United Nations: an organization of many countries, established to solve world problems

urban: relating to a city or town

Index

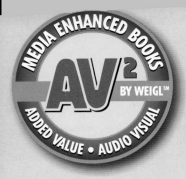

Log on to www.av2books.com

AV² by Weigl brings you media enhanced books that support active learning. Go to www.av2books.com, and enter the special code found on page 2 of this book. You will gain access to enriched and enhanced content that supplements and complements this book. Content includes video, audio, weblinks, quizzes, a slide show, and activities.

AV² Online Navigation

Book Pages
AV² pages directly correspond to pages in the book.

Key Words
Study vocabulary, and complete a matching word activity.

Quizzes
Test your knowledge.

Slide Show
View images and captions, and prepare a presentation.

Audio
Listen to sections of the book read aloud.

Video
Watch informative video clips.

Embedded Weblinks
Gain additional information for research.

Try This!
Complete activities and hands-on experiments.

AV² was built to bridge the gap between print and digital. We encourage you to tell us what you like and what you want to see in the future.

Sign up to be an AV² Ambassador at www.av2books.com/ambassador.